Happy Valentine's Day!

Other Books by
Carol Barkin and Elizabeth James

Happy Thanksgiving!

How to Be School Smart:
Secrets of Successful Schoolwork

How to Keep a Secret:
Writing and Talking in Code

How to Write a Great School Report

How to Write a Term Paper

How to Write Your Best Book Report

The Scary Halloween Costume Book

What Do You Mean by "Average"?
Means, Medians, and Modes

Happy Valentine's Day!

BY CAROL BARKIN
& ELIZABETH JAMES

pictures by Martha Weston

Lothrop, Lee & Shepard Books · New York

First Edition 1 2 3 4 5 6 7 8 9 10

Library of Congress Cataloging in Publication Data
Barkin, Carol. Happy Valentine's Day!
Summary: Presents a short history of Valentine's Day and includes recipes for appropriate foods and deserts and instructions for making Valentines and other decorations. 1. Saint Valentine's Day—Juvenile literature. 2. Recipes—Juvenile literature. 3. Greeting cards—Juvenile literature. [1. Valentine's Day. 2. Recipes. 3. Valentine decorations. 4. Handicraft] I. James, Elizabeth. II. Title. GT4925.B27 1988   394.2'683   87-35812
ISBN 0-688-06796-4   ISBN 0-688-06797-2 (lib. bdg.)

This is dedicated to the ones we love!

Contents

Why is lettuce the most loving vegetable?

Because it's all heart.

What do squirrels give for Valentine's Day?

Forget-me-nuts.

1· The Sweetest Day in the Year

Every February 14 people send cards to friends, family, and others they care about. Some even give little gifts as tokens of their affection. Why is this? Because it's Valentine's Day.

This happy holiday celebrates friendship, love, and romance. So everywhere you look you see hearts and cupids, flowers and lace—all these are traditional symbols of Valentine's Day. But it isn't just a holiday for sweethearts. It's a time to let all those special people in your life know how much you like them. This is what friendship is all about. And you can probably think of others who are important to you—moms and dads, grandparents and other family members, even teachers. Valentine's Day is a good time to tell them how you feel.

Valentine's Day has been a holiday for centuries, yet no one knows exactly where the name came from. It seems to have been named after an early Christian martyr, Saint Valentine. But which one was he? One legend says that he was a priest who performed secret marriages for young couples during the days when the Roman emperor Claudius II forbade soldiers to marry. Another story is that a priest named Valentine was jailed because he refused to pray to the Roman gods. While he was in jail he cured the blind daughter of the jailer. On the day of his execution he supposedly wrote her a farewell note and signed it, "From Your Valentine."

Is this where the tradition of sending cards and poems on Valentine's Day comes from? No one knows for sure. But it doesn't really matter how it got started.

Today it's a day of fun and friendship, of love and laughter.

What will you do to celebrate Valentine's Day this year? Perhaps you'll exchange cards with the other kids in your class. Maybe you'd like to create some special cards for those special friends or family members. And how about an easy-to-make gift for Mom or Dad or a yummy dessert for the holiday table? A friend might be giving a Valentine's Day party, or perhaps you'll decide to give one yourself. Whatever you do for the holiday, you'll find lots of great ideas in this book that will help you make it a fun and festive occasion.

Happy Valentine's Day!

What did the letter say to the stamp?

You send me.

What did the stamp say to the envelope?

I'm stuck on you.

2 · Be Mine, Valentine

Exchanging valentines is a popular custom. These cards express your feelings in many ways—silly or sentimental, funny or friendly, warm or totally wild. What a treat for your big sister or little brother to find a valentine specially made by you on the breakfast table. It's often hard to tell people how much you care about them, but a Valentine message can express your feelings perfectly.

13

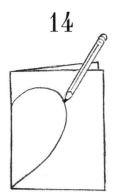

Or how about giving someone a "mystery" valentine? You don't always have to sign your name to the cards you send. If you feel shy, just sign yourself "A Secret Admirer." Remember that receiving valentines makes people feel good. It lets them know they are liked. And if you get a valentine from a "Mysterious Stranger," you'll see how much fun it is to try to guess who sent it.

· HOW TO MAKE A HEART ·

Since a heart is one of the most frequently used symbols of Valentine's Day, it's important to know how to make one. The simplest way is to start with a folded piece of paper. Draw half a heart shape out from the fold. Then cut it out and open it up. Doing it this way ensures that both halves, or sides, of the heart will be the same. The first couple of tries might not produce exactly the look you want, so use some scratch paper to practice. Once you have a heart you're happy with, use it as a pattern to trace around for your valentines.

But what if none of the hearts you make looks right? There is another method that's a little more work but that gives a perfect heart shape. You may want to make

this heart out of heavy paper or thin cardboard so you can keep the pattern and use it over and over.

The heart consists of two halves of a circle attached to the adjoining sides of a square. The sides of the square and the diameter of the circle need to be the same length.

Begin by making the circle. If you have a compass, your circle can be any size you want. But if not, trace around something circular like the rim of a glass or a can. Now cut out the circle, fold it down the center, and cut along the fold line to make two half circles. Measure the length of the straight edge—this is how long you want each side of the square to be.

Now measure and draw the square and cut it out. Here's a hint: When making your square, it's easiest to use one corner of a piece of paper for one corner of the square.

Attach your square and half circles with tape as shown in the drawing. You'll have a nice plump heart pattern that will help you make terrific valentines.

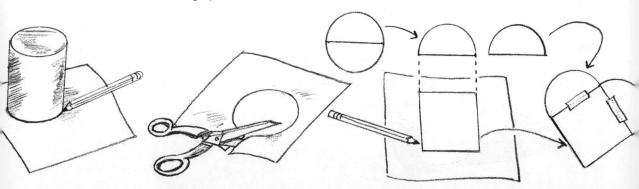

· RIBBONS AND LACE ·

What do you think of when someone mentions valentines? Red velvet hearts, satin and frilly lace, Cupid and his arrows of love? This is the traditional Valentine look, and it's a perfect one for Mom or Grandma. Making one of these old-fashioned valentines gives your imagination a chance to take off. Be as fancy and flowery as you want—the more trimmings the better.

You might want to start with the traditional basics of valentine making—red construction paper, white lacy paper doilies, stickers or cutouts of pretty flowers, hearts large and small. What else can you use?

Pretend you're on a scavenger hunt as you search for additional materials for your valentines. A good place to look in is the box of wrappings for Christmas and other occasions—you can usually find short pieces of red, pink, or white ribbon, and maybe some red tissue paper. If someone in your house sews, there's bound to be a box of fabric scraps as well as a collection of leftover bits of trimmings.

Here are a few of the items you might find around the house: lace seam binding, scraps of red fabric (keep your eyes open for velvet, satin, and other glamorous materials), pieces of ribbon, feathers, sequins and glitter, aluminum foil and other metallic paper, yarn in Valentine colors, pieces of old costume jewelry.

You'll no doubt come across other bits and pieces that will inspire some wonderful creations. Just make sure you don't use the fabric your aunt was saving for doll clothes—ask permission first.

Ordinary white glue will work fine for almost any small pieces you want to attach to your valentines. But before you begin making them, figure out if you can deliver them by hand or if you need to mail them. For those that will be mailed, it's a good idea to get the envelopes first and make your valentines the right size to slip inside. Manila envelopes come in many different sizes, so you can make large valentines if you want. And don't forget, cards that go through the mail should be fairly flat—glued-on glitter and things that stick out too much are likely to fall off before they reach their destination. Of course, for the valentines you deliver by hand, the sky's the limit.

Traditional Favorite

For a tried-and-true valentine that always looks pretty, you'll need red construction paper and paper doilies. Make a large red heart and glue a round doily on top of it. Add a second, smaller red heart and write your message across it in black.

This basic idea can be varied in lots of ways. Start with a whole sheet of red construction paper instead of a heart shape. Use doilies in different shapes and make more layers of alternating red and white. Cut the lace edge off a couple of doilies and glue these lace strips around the edge of the large red heart. Put a layer of metallic paper under the doily so the silver or gold shines through the lace pattern, or use metallic doilies. Add a gleaming design on the top layer with glued-on glitter or sequins. Or introduce another color to liven things up—hot or pale pink or even lavender can give extra pizzazz.

A Heart Full of Love

For a really special valentine that your mom or grandmother would love, here's an easy project that looks sensational. It's a heart-shaped pouf of padded fabric, trimmed with lace or ribbons.

First you need to cut a heart out of lightweight cardboard—the back of a writing pad or the kind of cardboard that comes in shirts works fine. This will be the base of the valentine. Make it about six inches across or more because smaller ones are hard to work with.

Now select the fabric. It should be lightweight and not stiff. Silky polyester lining material is great, and so is thin velour or cotton. You could use plain red or pink, or a pretty print of small flowers. Cut out a heart from the fabric—it should be about one inch larger than the cardboard heart all the way around.

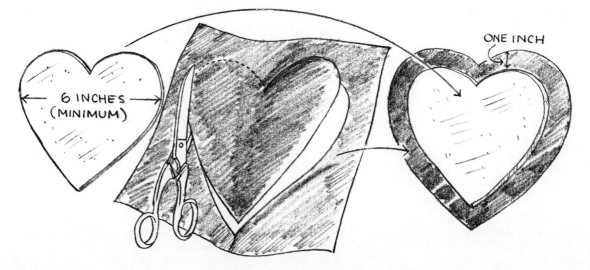

6 INCHES (MINIMUM)

ONE INCH

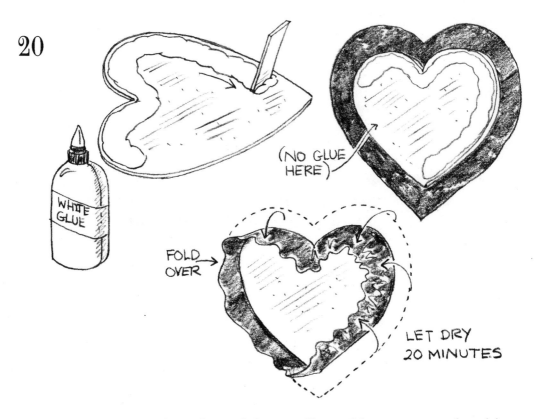

(NO GLUE HERE)

FOLD OVER →

LET DRY 20 MINUTES

WHITE GLUE

On the edge of the cardboard heart, spread a thin coat of white glue around the two top humps and along one side down to the point. Center the heart on the wrong side of the fabric heart, glue side up. Now fold the fabric edge over and press it down carefully. (Your fingers may get a little sticky but don't worry—the glue will wash off.)

Let the glue dry for twenty minutes or so. Then turn the heart over. Tear paper towels or facial tissues into strips about two or three inches wide and crumple them loosely. Push one strip at a time into the heart, making sure to get some stuffing into the upper corners. You don't have to pack it too full—just enough to make it look puffed out.

When your valentine is stuffed, turn it over and spread glue along the open edge of the cardboard. Then fold over the remaining fabric edge and press it down to seal the heart closed. Let this glued section dry.

Now you're ready to decorate. If you're handy with needle and thread, you can sew an edging of lace seam binding all around the front edge of the heart. Take little tucks to make it fit around the curves.

It's almost impossible to glue lace seam binding, however, so if you aren't good at sewing, try tying the lace into little bows. These can be pinned on with small gold safety pins or attached with a stitch or two. Or do the same thing with pretty satin or velvet ribbon bows.

If you came across a string of old fake pearls or a discarded pin covered with glittery fake jewels, try pinning or stitching it onto the heart fabric. Experiment with different arrangements. Maybe you can twist the fake pearls together with a piece of ribbon and drape it across the heart. End it in a fancy ribbon bow.

For the final touch, write your Valentine message on a small piece of white paper and pin it to the center of your padded heart with a little safety pin.

You can make the same kind of padded heart valentine for Dad or Grandpa. But this time you'll want something that's not so frilly. Why not look for a piece of an old striped or checked shirt or some plain or

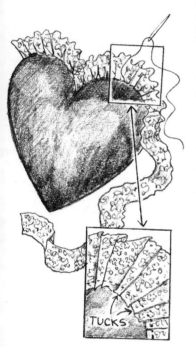

TUCKS

plaid flannel? Or you might use a piece of burlap for an outdoorsy look. Instead of ribbon and pearls, try using yarn bows, twine, or even shoelaces. If the valentine is for a sports fan, use fabric and yarn in his favorite team's colors and pin on a drawing or cutout of the team emblem.

· VALENTINES ACROSS THE MILES ·

You'll probably want to send valentines to people who live far away—relatives you're especially fond of, old friends who've moved out of town, pals you met at summer camp. These people haven't seen you for a while, so they'd really appreciate a valentine that includes a recent picture of you. But don't just sling a snapshot into the envelope before you seal it shut. Make your photo the key ingredient in a valentine you create yourself.

If you use thin cardboard for your valentine, it will be stiff enough to go through the mail without bending. But if you use construction paper, cut a rectangle or square of cardboard the size of the envelope to slip in along with the card and photo and keep them from being bent.

Peekaboo Photo Valentine

This rectangular card can be made to fit into almost any size envelope for easy mailing. In addition to the envelope, you need a rectangle of construction paper or thin colored cardboard, a round lacy paper doily, and, of course, a picture of yourself—make sure it's smaller than the construction paper rectangle.

Cut out an oval or heart shape in the middle of the construction paper card, as shown in the drawing. Make sure the hole is big enough for your face to show through, and then tape or glue your photo behind it.

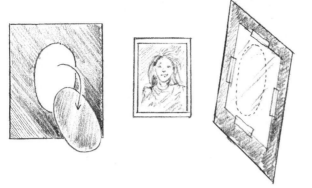

Now write your Valentine message above, below, or even around your picture.

Using your rectangle as a pattern, cut out a triangular piece from the edge of the doily, as shown in the drawing. Then cut three more pieces the same size.

Glue or tape the four doily pieces to the corners of your card on the front. They will overlap a little in the middle. And these "petals" will open up like a lacy white flower to reveal your Valentine message.

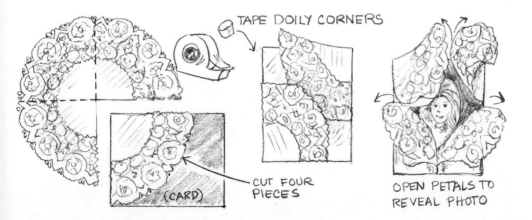

TAPE DOILY CORNERS

CUT FOUR PIECES

(CARD)

OPEN PETALS TO REVEAL PHOTO

Keepsake Valentine

To make this kind of photo valentine, you'll need a construction paper heart, an envelope big enough to hold it, and a picture that fits inside the heart. The best photo to use is either a wallet-size school picture of you or a snapshot of you and the person you're sending the valentine to.

On the back of the photo, be sure to write your

name along with the date and place where the picture was taken. Then lay the photograph on the heart and mark where the corners are. With a small sharp scissors, cut short diagonal slits in the heart to fit the photo corners into. Write your message on the front of the heart.

Grandma will be thrilled to receive this thoughtful valentine. She may want to hang the whole thing on the wall because the heart acts as a frame around the photograph. But maybe she'll prefer to remove the picture and keep it in her wallet. Then she can show it to all her friends.

· VALENTINES GO TO SCHOOL ·

You will no doubt want to give valentines to your friends at school. Maybe there's a valentine mailbox and you plan to have a valentine for everyone in your class. But you won't want to give out soppy sentimental cards to all your school friends. And there's no reason why you have to buy ones that are just like everyone else's. Why not try something different for a change?

Easy-Print Valentines

For this project you need some plain white paper (like typing paper), a small sponge you can cut up, red poster paint and a flat pan to pour it into, and stickers or tape to hold your cards closed. These are folded valentines, and one good way to begin is to cut the pieces of 8½-by-11-inch paper in half and then fold those pieces in half. Make as many of these folded cards as you need.

Cut the sponge into a heart shape that will fit on the front of the card. (Trace a heart with felt-tip marker on a damp sponge and then use scissors to cut it out.) Pour a little of the poster paint into an old aluminum pie pan or other flat, disposable container. Then dip

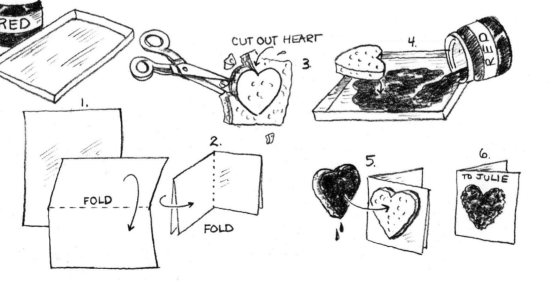

one side of the sponge heart into the paint and press it on the front of one of the cards to print a red heart shape. The printed heart will have a textured look because of the uneven surface of the sponge. If the paint seems too thick, add a drop or two of water to it.

When you've printed the fronts of all the cards, let them dry completely. Then use red felt-tip pen or crayon to write your message on the inside of the card. The words "Happy Valentine's Day" and your signature are fine. But you may decide to write a clever rhyme or Valentine joke or riddle instead and keep your name a secret.

These cards don't need envelopes, but of course they do need names so they can be delivered to the right people. So write each person's name on the front of a card, either in the white space or across the middle of the heart. Be sure you use black or some other color that will show up against the red.

Now your cards are ready to be taped shut. If you can get heart-shaped stickers, use those to seal your valentines. But other kinds of stickers will work fine, and so will plain transparent tape.

The Amazing Edible Valentine

If you're in the mood to make some really funny and fantastic valentines that your friends will talk about for the rest of the year, this is for you. Remember the silly vegetable jokes, like "My heart *beets* for you," that are on inexpensive valentines? These jokes have been around forever, but you're going to give them a new twist. Instead of cartoony pictures of the vegetables, your valentines are going to have the real thing.

First pick out the jokes you want to use. Here are some good ones, but you may come up with others you like better.

Do you *carrot* all for me?
Lettuce be Valentines.
I've *bean* hoping you'll be my Valentine.
Orange you going to be my Valentine?
I'm *nuts* about you.
There's a good *raisin* to be my Valentine.
Olive you, Valentine.
Peas be mine, Valentine.

For each valentine you're giving, make a construction paper heart large enough to write the joke on.

Don't forget to add the name of the person the valentine is for and your signature—you want to make sure you get credit for these terrific valentines.

Now comes the fun part. You need a sandwich bag for each valentine. Inside the bag place a small amount of the "joke" food: a couple of pieces of cut-up carrot, a leaf of lettuce, one or two string beans, a slice of orange (leave the skin on), a small handful of nuts or raisins, an olive or two, or a few peas.

Fold over the top of each bag and staple the heart to it—make sure the staples go through the folded part so the bag doesn't come open. Hand out these valentines at school and watch the looks of amazement on your friends' faces.

A similar kind of funny valentine can be made with gum. Choose the kind that comes in sticks with individual paper wrappers, and try to get some that has pink wrapping for a Valentine look. Make a construction paper heart for each valentine and write on each one, "Won't *chew* be my Valentine?"

Underneath the joke, spread a little bit of glue and then press on one wrapped stick of gum. Or use a piece of clear tape to hold the gum on the heart.

Whatever kinds of valentines you choose to make, you can be sure that your family and friends will be thrilled to get them. They'll be delighted to discover how much you care. And their happiness will make you feel good too.

What is a vampire's sweetheart called?

His ghoul-friend.

Why did the banana go out with the prune?

Because it couldn't get a date.

·3· Hearts and Flowers and Pretty Presents

Nobody really expects to get presents on Valentine's Day, but very few people are upset when they receive a gift! You might want to give something to the special people in your life, whether they are relatives, neighbors you're close to, or "best friends." Valentine gifts don't need to be expensive or elaborate. They're meant to be tokens of your affection. And the thought and care you put into a handmade present makes it extra special.

The Valentine presents you'll find in this chapter are pretty things that are also practical. After you've tried them, you'll probably come up with lots of variations and new ideas on your own. And they're all super easy to make. Creating these gifts for people you love is part of celebrating Valentine's Day—invite a friend or two to share the fun of making them!

· A VALENTINE FOR READERS ·

Do you have a friend whose nose is always buried in a mystery? Or does your mom get frazzled every time she loses her place in the cookbook? Maybe your uncle loves biographies and is usually in the middle of two or three different books at one time. All these people need bookmarks!

Here's an easy way to make a useful and attractive place-saver for all the readers in your life. All you need are red construction paper, ribbon, and white glue. (If you happen to have a little bit of red felt around, you can use that instead of construction paper.)

Cut two hearts the same size from the construction paper—a good size to use is about 2 inches high and 2½ inches wide. (You might have a heart-shaped cookie cutter the right size to use as a pattern.) Then cut a piece of ribbon about 12 inches long. You can use any color ribbon that goes with the red hearts.

Put down some newspaper or wax paper to work on. Now spread a thin coating of white glue all over one of the hearts. Lay about one-half inch of one end of the ribbon on the heart as in the drawing, and then place the other heart on top. Press the two hearts together with a crumpled piece of paper towel to squeeze out the excess glue. Let the hearts dry.

Cut the end of the ribbon at a diagonal to make a pretty finish. When the bookmark is used, the heart hangs over the front of the book as an attractive decoration and a reminder of the nice person who gave it.

WHITE GLUE

12 INCH RIBBON

2 INCHES

2½ INCHES

· NIFTY NOTEPAPER ·

There's hardly anybody in the world who wouldn't be delighted to have some pretty notepaper to write letters on. And this project is a lot of fun to do. You'll need plain white typewriter paper, white glue, and red tissue paper to make the notecards. In most large supermarkets and stationery stores you can buy inexpensive envelopes that measure 3⅝ by 6½ inches, so you can give some lucky person a set of fancy notes and matching envelopes.

First trim off a strip 1½ inches wide from one long edge of the paper. Then fold the paper in quarters to make a notecard that measures 5½ by 3½ inches.

Now cut out a 5½-by-3½-inch rectangle of red tissue paper. Fold it into quarters and then at an angle, as shown. Make heart shapes by cutting out half hearts along the folded edges, the same way you make a snowflake from folded paper. Experiment a few times to see how the patterns turn out.

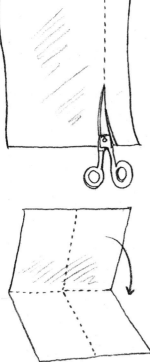

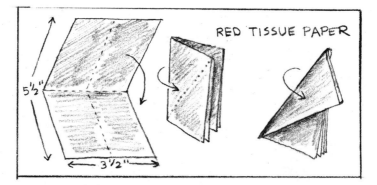

RED TISSUE PAPER

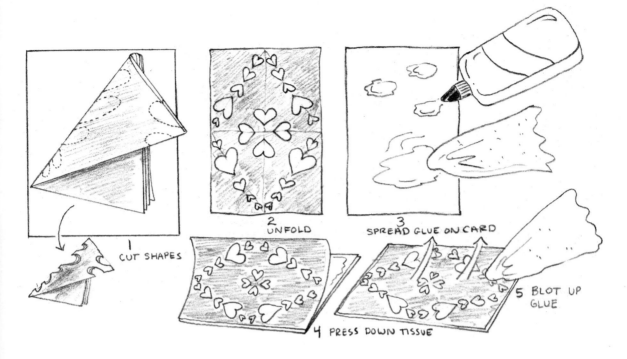

1 CUT SHAPES

2 UNFOLD

3 SPREAD GLUE ON CARD

4 PRESS DOWN TISSUE

5 BLOT UP GLUE

When you have a cutout rectangle you like, glue it onto the front of your notecard. The best way to do this is to put a few drops of white glue on the notepaper. Using a crumpled paper towel, spread the glue all over the card in a thin layer. Then lay one long edge of your tissue paper cutout along the folded edge of the notecard and press it down gently. Smooth the rest of the tissue paper carefully across the front of the notecard. Press it down and blot up excess glue with a crumpled paper towel.

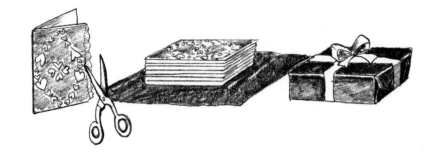

Let the notepaper dry. If the tissue paper hangs over the edges, trim it off; but be cautious—you don't want to cut the notepaper. Depending on how much glue you use, a few of your cards may warp a little. Once the glue is completely dry and you've trimmed any excess tissue paper off the edges, you can press the cards flat between two heavy books.

Package four or six notecards with the same number of envelopes and wrap the set in more of the red tissue paper. Tie it up with a pretty ribbon and you've got a great gift for your Valentine.

· PERSONALIZED LETTER HOLDER ·

Here's a handy catchall for those letters that need to be answered soon. It looks pretty and keeps papers organized so they can be found when they're needed. Smooth and sleek, the heart shape goes with any

décor—you could even make two, one for Mom's desk and one for Dad's.

For each letter holder, you need some corrugated cardboard (a piece of a cardboard carton) and some lightweight red cardboard. (Depending on which store you go to, the lightweight cardboard will be called railroad board, oaktag, or poster board. Just make sure it's thin enough so you can cut it with a pair of scissors. It has a smooth, slightly shiny surface.)

On a piece of scratch paper, trace around the rim of a saucer or butter plate and cut out the circle. Cut it in half and then draw a square on the scratch paper, making the sides of the square the same length as the straight edge of the half circle. Cut out the square.

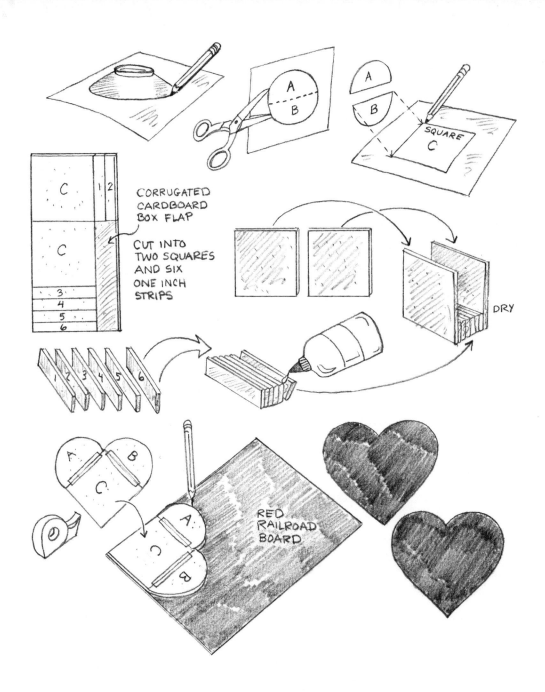

CORRUGATED
CARDBOARD
BOX FLAP

CUT INTO
TWO SQUARES
AND SIX
ONE INCH
STRIPS

DRY

SQUARE
C

RED
RAILROAD
BOARD

Using the square as a pattern, draw and cut out two pieces of corrugated cardboard. (If you start at a corner of a box flap, you'll only need to cut two sides of each cardboard square.) Then cut six strips of corrugated cardboard as long as one side of the squares and about an inch wide. Glue the strips together in a stack using white glue. This will be the base of the letter holder. If you happen to have or find a piece of 1-by-1-inch or 1-by-2-inch wood (like a scrap from the lumberyard) that's about the right length, you can use that instead.

Sandwich the stack of strips (or piece of wood) between the cardboard squares so that they are all lined up along one edge. Glue this "sandwich" together with white glue too, wiping off any excess with a paper towel. This needs to dry before you can complete the project. It's a good idea to lay it flat between two sheets of wax paper and rest a heavy book on top of the base to compress the stack while it dries.

Meanwhile, tape the scratch paper heart pattern together. Using a corner of the red railroad board as a starting point for the tip of the heart, carefully trace and cut out a red heart. You need two of these, so trace and cut out another one.

44 Spread white glue all over the outsides of the two corrugated cardboard squares and attach the red hearts as shown in the drawing. This also needs to be surrounded by wax paper, weighted down, and left to dry for an hour or so. Slip a couple of old magazines or paperback books into the letter holder before putting the heavy book on top so that the holder isn't crushed together.

Once the glue is dry, it's time to personalize your Valentine letter holder. For Dad, how about a nice plaid effect made with strips of colored tape or just his initials in big block lettering? For your aunt who plays

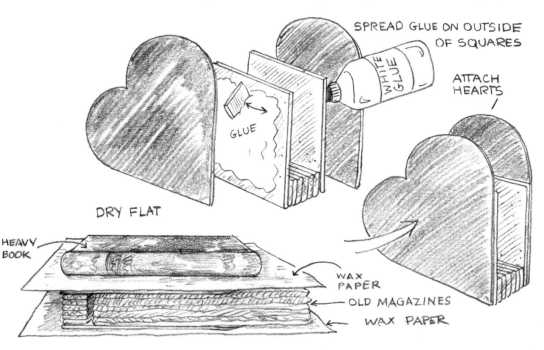

SPREAD GLUE ON OUTSIDE OF SQUARES

WHITE GLUE

ATTACH HEARTS

GLUE

DRY FLAT

HEAVY BOOK

WAX PAPER

OLD MAGAZINES

WAX PAPER

Scrabble by mail, you might want to photocopy part of a page in a dictionary and glue that to the letter holder. Think about the person you're giving your valentine to and choose some small decoration that reflects his or her interests. For a gourmet cook you could cut out the picture of a chef's hat from a magazine and paste it on the heart, or for a stamp collector you might get a whole bunch of one-cent and two-cent stamps and make a collage out of them to cover the letter holder. Whatever you decide on, this Valentine gift is sure to be a hit!

· VICTORIAN VALENTINE NECKLACE ·

This short necklace fits snugly around the throat, a style that used to be called a choker (not a very pretty name for this old-fashioned, romantic addition to any girl's Valentine's Day outfit!). A cameo brooch on a black velvet ribbon was a popular look a hundred years ago. But you can make your Valentine choker out of any kind of ribbon you like. Just make sure it's long enough to tie in a bow at the back of your neck. Of course, you can use velvet ribbon in black or any other color. But what about trying lace seam binding

to create a delicate look or brightly colored satin ribbon for some shiny pizzazz?

For a Valentine necklace, you'll want a heart as the centerpiece. A super easy way to get this great look is with stickers. There are lots to choose from—red and white traditional, fluorescent day-glow for a night of fun, stripes for sports, or whatever matches the person you're giving it to. Get two and put them back to back over the middle of the ribbon necklace. If you like, you can create a "chain of hearts" by adding stickers to each side of the center one. However you design this necklace, it will be a terrific addition to your Valentine's wardrobe.

· SWEETS TO THE SWEET ·

Perhaps you have seen the heart-shaped boxes of chocolates that appear in stores every February. For years this was the traditional Valentine gift from a young man to his sweetheart. But these days sweets aren't just for sweethearts. Anyone on your list will be delighted to receive a batch of homemade goodies. Make it a double gift—pack your treats in a beautiful and unusual container that will be treasured for years to come.

mold

The gift container for your Valentine sweets is made of papier-mâché. It's a very easy process but it is a little messy, so be sure to work on several layers of newspaper to protect the table or the floor.

First, find a bowl or serving dish to use as a mold. One that's fairly shallow and not too large is best.

For the papier-mâché, tear newspaper into strips about one inch wide. You'll need enough to make many layers of paper all over the bowl, so make lots of strips—you may end up with leftovers but that's better than having to stop in the middle to make more.

For the paste, mix together 1 cup of flour, 2 cups of cold water, and about 2 tablespoonfuls of white

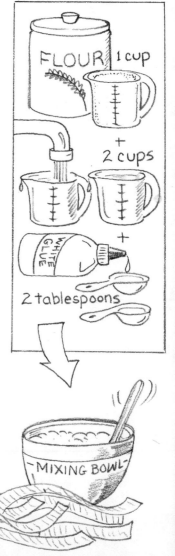

FLOUR 1 cup

+
2 cups

WHITE GLUE

2 tablespoons

MIXING BOWL

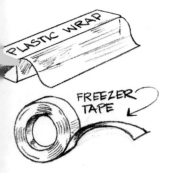

glue in a medium-sized mixing bowl. You can stir it with a fork to get the lumps out.

You'll also need a piece of plastic wrap and some masking or freezer tape as well as pieces of red and white gift-wrap and more white glue.

On your newspaper-covered work surface, turn the dish you are using for a mold upside down and cover it with a sheet of plastic wrap. Tape the edges of the plastic wrap to the inside of the bowl so it doesn't slide off as you work.

Dip one strip of newspaper into the paste, coating it completely; holding it over the paste bowl, run your finger and thumb along it to get rid of excess paste; then lay the wet strip across the mold and press it

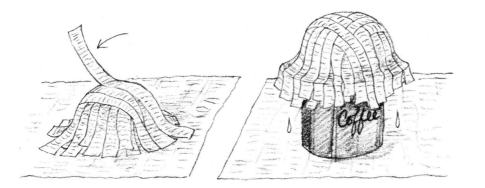

down smoothly. Continue to add more strips, covering the mold completely and as evenly as you can. The strips should go in all directions to build up strong layers. Make sure the ends of the newspaper strips extend past the rim of the bowl, but don't worry about making the edge neat right now—you'll trim off the uneven ends later when it's dry.

When you've used up all the paste, the papier-mâché is finished. Lift the whole thing, including the mold, carefully and put it in a warm place to dry. It's a good idea to set the mold on a coffee can or something similar to let the air get under it—the can will look as if it's wearing a weird hat. Papier-mâché seems to take forever to dry; let your container sit for at least two days to dry completely.

When the papier-mâché is dry, separate it carefully from the mold and remove the plastic wrap if it's stuck. Use an old pair of scissors (not the good ones) to trim the edge of your container, making it as smooth as you can. But don't worry about the lumps and bumps in the surface of the container—that's part of the handmade look.

To give your papier-mâché bowl a pretty Valentine finish, cover it with a torn-paper collage. Any kind of red and white gift-wrapping paper will look great. Use a pattern with hearts or flowers, red and white stripes, or anything else you like. Cut a piece of gift-wrap that looks big enough to wrap up your bowl and tear this into small pieces about one by two inches or so. They don't have to be neat, but don't make them too tiny to handle easily.

You'll need a way to spread the white glue on the backs of the pieces of torn paper. You could pour some glue into a disposable pan and use a brush to

-RIM FIRST-   - THEN INSIDE -   LET DRY

-THEN OUTSIDE-

WHITE GLUE

spread it, or you can dribble some glue onto each piece and smoosh it around with a crumpled paper towel. Either way, it's a messy job, but it's also a lot of fun.

Wrap the torn paper, one piece at a time, over the rim of the papier-mâché container. Overlap the edges so all the newspaper gets covered up, and press each piece down so the glue spreads out and squeezes under the edges.

After the whole rim is covered, work on the inside of the container. The torn paper won't lie completely flat, but it's supposed to have little wrinkles in it. Just make sure you use enough glue to hold all the paper down. (The glue dries clear, so it won't show.) When the inside is finished, turn the container over and do the outside.

Before you set your container aside to dry, look it over carefully. Smear some extra glue (with your fingers—it will wash off) on any edges that are sticking up, and check to see that all the newspaper is covered. Then let the whole thing sit for a couple of hours to dry.

What kind of goodies will you put in this Valentine container? If you have a favorite recipe for fudge or

cookies or something else that's delicious, make up a batch. Or try this fast and foolproof way of making tasty heart-shaped cookies.

Start with a package of refrigerated peanut butter or sugar cookie dough—it comes in a tube-shaped package wrapped in plastic in the refrigerated section of the market. Remove the plastic packaging and wrap the cookie dough in wax paper. Put it in the freezer for a couple of hours—this makes the dough firmer and a little easier to work with.

Cut or break off a piece of dough about the size of a walnut. Flatten it with your fingers and lay it on a cookie sheet. Push it into a heart shape as neatly as you can. (The package says the tube of dough will make three dozen cookies, but if you don't end up with that many, don't worry. Just make sure to leave enough space between the raw cookies so they can expand as they bake.)

If you like, dot the cookies with red-hot cinnamon hearts or other baking decorations. Then bake them according to the directions on the package—make sure you have an adult's help when lighting or using the oven.

When the cookies are completely cool, you're ready

to package your gift. Fill the papier-mâché bowl with your sweet treats. Then set it in the middle of a large piece of tissue paper and pull up all the corners of the paper to make a loose, rounded wrapping. Use contrasting ribbon to tie the ends together on top of the container in a pretty bow. This is a really outstanding present to give to someone you love.

· MAKE A MESSAGE TO WEAR ·

Everyone loves to wear T-shirts with funny or intriguing messages, and here's a chance to make one for a special friend. You can get inexpensive white T-shirts at discount stores—they usually come in packages of two or three, so you can make one for yourself too! You may want to buy extra-roomy shirts so they can be worn over a turtleneck or leotard on Valentine's Day.

Wash the T-shirts before you start making your designs on them. They may shrink a little in the dryer. Then draw your design or message on the T-shirt with pencil. You might make a necklace—a large heart in the center and a row of smaller hearts going up to the neck of the T-shirt. Or, for a boy, how about a necktie decorated with hearts and stars or question marks?

When you're happy with your design, you're ready to make it permanent. Of course, you can use regular fabric pens made for drawing on cloth—they come in lots of different colors. But there are special "pens" that make designs that stand out from the fabric. You can get three different kinds—a slick plastic look, a fuzzy look, and a glitter look. The pens themselves are squat squeeze tubes with plastic nozzles. If you can find these in an art supply, fabric, or novelty store, they're even more fun to use than regular fabric pens.

Lay the T-shirt flat and slide a piece of cardboard between the front and back to keep the color from going through. Work slowly and carefully because the

color is permanent and won't wash out. (If you make a mistake, turn it into part of your design by adding an extra heart or other shape—no one will know it wasn't meant to be that way.)

Keep the shirt flat for several hours to let it dry completely. If you plan to add designs to both front and back, leave enough time for the first side to dry before turning the shirt over.

To wrap your T-shirt, fold it neatly and then roll it up into a tube shape. Use tissue paper or other Valentine paper that is four or five inches wider than the rolled-up T-shirt. Wrap it around the tube shape and tie the ends with ribbon or yarn to make the package look like a firecracker. What a great surprise for a friend on Valentine's Day!

What did the light bulb say to the switch?

You turn me on.

Did Adam and Eve ever have a date?

No, but they had an apple.

4 · *Valentine Treats and Eats*

Valentine's Day is a great excuse for making fun foods that have a flavor of the day. Sweets, of course, are traditional Valentine favorites, but so are red or pink foods and heart-shaped treats.

As you look through these recipes, you'll discover lots of tasty "valentines" to eat. Some, like the Mini-Heart Sandwiches and Ribbon Sandwiches, will be great additions to your school class's Valentine's Day celebration. Prepare them the night before and be sure to make enough for everyone—these yummy treats will go fast. And, of course, the pink heart-shaped cake will be the perfect ending to the classroom feast. Just be sure to carry it to school on a cookie sheet or a piece of heavy cardboard so you don't end up with a broken heart.

For a Valentine's Day party at home, you can choose any of these holiday foods that appeal to you. Why not make a dessert bar with a selection of delicious desserts and drinks for your friends to sample? And you'll find lots of other party ideas in the next chapter.

Of course, the whole point of Valentine's Day is to let the people you care about know how you feel. What better way to tell the cook in your house how much you appreciate him or her than to make a Valentine meal yourself? This "cook's night off" is a great gift, and it's also fun for you to create a Valentine menu.

Write the menu in your fanciest handwriting on a red or white paper heart and decorate it however you like. Then present it to Mom or Dad on Valentine's Day morning. The whole family will love the special fun foods you prepare, and everyone will look forward to coming up with new variations for next year. This gift might turn into a new family tradition!

· STARTERS ·

These snacks are great before dinner as appetizers, and they're also just the thing to munch during a study break or while you watch a game on TV. The Mini-Heart Sandwiches and the Valentine Veggies pack well, so you can take them to school or to a Scout meeting.

Mini-Heart Sandwiches

These one-bite sandwiches are so easy to eat, you'll have to make lots!

    sliced bread
    cream cheese and red food coloring OR
        sliced bologna and cheese
    heart-shaped cookie cutter

To make pink cream cheese, mix a drop or two of red food coloring into two to four ounces of cream cheese. If it's too stiff to blend, add a little milk and stir well.

For open-face sandwiches, spread a slice of bread with a thin layer of pink cream cheese. Use the cookie cutter to cut out as many heart shapes as you can from each slice. If you like, decorate each sandwich with a thin slice of radish or red pepper.

For double-face mini-sandwiches, use the cookie cutter to cut out several hearts of bread and bologna or sliced cheese (or both). Stack them together—you can combine the fillings or keep them separate. If you like mustard or mayonnaise, spread these on the bread before putting the sandwiches together.

Golden Hearts

Here's a variation on the heart-shaped sandwiches. Everyone at your house will love these hot, tasty tidbits on a cold February evening.

sliced bread
sliced cheese
paprika
heart-shaped cookie cutter

Use the cookie cutter to make enough bread hearts for the group you're feeding. Then cut the same number of hearts from sliced cheese—whatever kind your family likes best.

Put the bread hearts on a baking sheet and lay a cheese heart on top of each one. If you like, sprinkle each one with a bit of paprika for a rosy glow.

Turn on the broiler (be sure you have an adult's permission or help) and put the golden hearts in for three to five minutes to let the cheese melt. Then take them out and serve right away.

Valentine Veggies

A plate of raw vegetables is a great starter or accompaniment to any meal. Look for vegetables with natural red coloring, such as radishes, tomatoes (especially cherry tomatoes), red peppers, and cooked beets, and for white vegetables, like raw cauliflower, onion slices, or peeled cucumber.

    red vegetables
    white vegetables
    celery
    cream cheese and red food coloring

Cut the vegetables into attractive pieces—spears, rounds, or slices. For stuffed celery, mix a small amount of cream cheese with a drop of red food coloring and spread this pink cream cheese in the hollow part of each celery stalk.

Arrange the vegetables on a serving plate. It's fun to plan an attractive pattern, such as alternating the red vegetables with the white ones and the stuffed celery. Or you might start out with a heart of red pepper slices in the center, surrounded by a layer of thin cucumber rounds topped with half cherry tomatoes. Let your imagination go and you'll end up with a plate of nutritious goodies that's almost too pretty to eat.

· MAIN COURSES ·

These are perfect for a Valentine's Day lunch or supper. Choose between dainty Ribbon Sandwiches and casual Heart-y Pizza, or make both and let everyone sample a little of each.

Pink Ribbon Sandwiches

Ribbon sandwiches have been around for a long time. Your mom and your grandmother may remember nibbling them at fancy luncheons or afternoon tea parties. Of course they're not made out of ribbons. They're fun to put together and even more fun to eat, and they have just the right look for a Valentine's Day meal.

very thin sliced bread—white, whole wheat, or both

sandwich fillings, such as—

- pink cream cheese: Add 2 drops of red food coloring to about 4 ounces of cream cheese. If you use regular cream cheese instead of the whipped kind, add a little milk to make it spread more easily.
- deviled ham: This canned spread has a nice pink color that looks attractive in the ribbon sandwiches.
- blended cheeses: Mix ½ cup of cottage cheese, ½ cup of ricotta cheese, and ¼ cup (2 ounces) of feta or blue cheese in the blender or food processor (ask an adult's permission or help). You can add some garlic powder and some pepper if you want. Scoop it out of the processor and then stir in some chopped red pepper for color—or leave it plain white if you prefer.
- peanut butter and jelly: Be sure to use red jelly in this old standby.
- bologna or other lunch meat
- thin-sliced tomatoes and cucumbers

Ribbon sandwiches start with layered stacks of
bread and fillings. Get out five slices of thin sandwich
bread; lay them on top of one another and slice off all
the crusts. Now spread four slices of the bread with
whatever fillings you've chosen. Each one can be different or you can alternate two kinds of filling, like
pink cream cheese and bologna. Then stack them up,
finishing with a plain piece of bread. Wrap the stack in
wax paper or plastic wrap and put it in the refrigerator
for an hour or so—this makes it easier to slice.

When the sandwich stack is cold, take it out and use
a very sharp knife to slice it into four equal strips. Be
cautious with the knife and ask permission before
using it. When you lay the sandwich slices on their
sides, the stripes of filling and bread will look like
different colored ribbons.

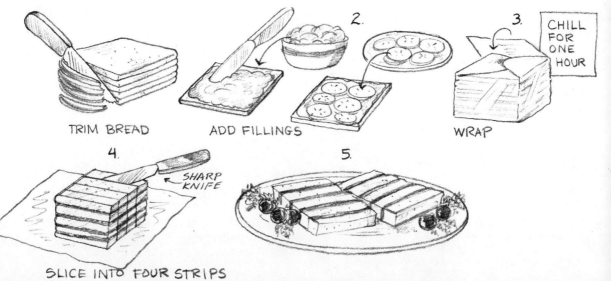

1. TRIM BREAD

2. ADD FILLINGS

3. WRAP — CHILL FOR ONE HOUR

4. SLICE INTO FOUR STRIPS — SHARP KNIFE

5.

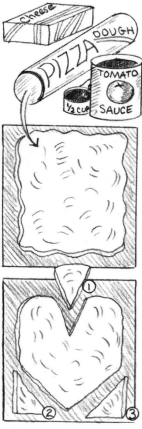

Heart-y Pizza

Just about everybody loves pizza, and you'll be surprised to find out how much fun it is to make your own. It's easy to do and your family and friends will be impressed when you bring it out hot from the oven.

package of ready-made pizza dough
½ cup of tomato sauce
6–8 ounces of cheese
extras (see page 67)

You can find ready-made pizza dough in the supermarket's refrigerated section—it comes in a cardboard tube. One package makes a pizza that will serve four hungry people.

Naturally, a Valentine pizza has to be the right shape! Unroll the rectangle of pizza dough on a cookie sheet. With a table knife, slice off the bottom corners of the dough and cut a triangle out of the center top. Use your hands to mold the dough into a heart shape. Then cut the extra dough into thin strips and attach them around the edges to make a rim.

Now spread the tomato sauce on the dough—spaghetti sauce or canned tomato sauce mixed with a little oregano and basil works well.

CUT EXTRA DOUGH INTO STRIPS FOR RIM

You can use mozzarella cheese for the traditional pizza flavor, or any combination of cheeses you like, such as cheddar, Monterey jack, Munster, or even Swiss. Buy it grated or grate it yourself—be careful not to skin your knuckles.

What do you like on your pizza? Here are some ideas:

- Peppers—slices of red or green pepper look attractive and add a little zing.
- Mushrooms—use canned mushrooms in slices or small pieces, or slice up a few fresh ones and distribute them on top of the cheese.
- Salami—add slices of any salami (this includes pepperoni) for extra flavor.
- Olives, anchovies, onions—if you and your friends like these pizza toppings, scatter some over the grated cheese.

Bake the pizza according to the directions on the package (ask an adult for help or for permission to use the oven). The pizza will be done in about twenty to twenty-five minutes, so plan to have everyone gathered at the table when you bring it out hot and bubbling in its Valentine crust.

· DESSERTS ·

Almost any kind of dessert can be turned into a Valentine treat if you add something red or pink to it, like cherries or strawberries. But here are a few ideas for special endings to your Valentine's Day meals. Combine them any way you like for sweets everyone will enjoy.

Rosy Applesauce

This is an incredibly easy way to give an ordinary food a special Valentine look.

8-ounce jar of applesauce
red food coloring

Just add three or four drops of food coloring to the applesauce and stir it well. The applesauce will turn a beautiful rosy pink color. Serve it in pretty bowls as a dessert or a side dish for the Valentine dinner.

Valentine Surprise Pudding

Nothing could be simpler to make than this great-tasting pudding. If you have four stemmed glasses you can use instead of bowls, your pudding will look especially elegant, but pretty dessert dishes will do fine.

1 package of vanilla instant pudding mix
2 cups of milk
½–1 cup of pitted canned or frozen
    cherries
red food coloring
whipped cream

Cut the cherries into halves or quarters, saving four whole ones to decorate the top of your individual servings. Mix up the pudding with milk according to package directions and add four or five drops of food coloring, a drop or two at a time. Stir in the cut-up cherries and spoon the pudding into the four dishes. Place a whole cherry on top of each and refrigerate until it's time to serve dessert. For an added dash of glamour, squirt a swirl of whipped cream around the cherry on each dish.

Old-Time Favorites

Gelatin desserts are practically everyone's favorites, and there are almost as many ways of fixing them as there are people. For Valentine's Day you'll want one of the red flavors—raspberry, strawberry, cherry, or mixed berry.

Favorite #1

1 package of gelatin dessert
water
fruit

For an extra-healthy and delicious dessert or side dish, you can use cut-up fresh fruit, like apples and bananas and oranges, in the gelatin along with some pieces of broken walnuts. Follow the package directions for making the gelatin and adding the fruit. Don't use fresh or frozen pineapple or kiwi—the gelatin won't jell if you do. And, of course, canned fruit works well too.

Favorite #2

1 package of gelatin dessert
water
⅓–½ cup of yogurt, plain or fruited
4 individual dessert dishes or glasses

For this layered delight, use 1¾ cups of water instead of 2 cups to make the gelatin. When the gelatin is dissolved, divide half of the mixture among the four dishes and pour the other half into a bowl to jell. Put the dishes and the bowl into the refrigerator and wait for the gelatin to set (this usually takes an hour or so).

Add the yogurt to the bowl of gelatin. With a wire whisk or a hand eggbeater, mix up the gelatin and yogurt just until the colors all go together. (Don't overdo or it will turn into liquid.) Pour this mixture on top of the clear gelatin in the four dessert dishes. Then put them back into the refrigerator until serving time.

DIVIDE GELATIN MIXTURE IN HALF

ADD YOGURT TO BOWL. MIX

ADD TO SERVING BOWLS. CHILL

Favorite #3

2 packages of gelatin dessert
water
heart-shaped or other mold
fruit and whipped cream for decoration

For a refreshing dessert that's very pretty to look at, make a gelatin mold. Since it's Valentine's Day, a heart-shaped mold would be nice, but any shape will do. Many molds hold two packages of gelatin, so measure your mold by pouring cups of plain water into it before you start mixing. Remember that for molded gelatin you use only 1¾ cups of water instead of 2 for each package. So if your mold holds 3½ cups of water, you'll need to make two packages of gelatin.

When you put the mold full of gelatin into the refrigerator, make sure it sits flat on the shelf—you want the finished product to look even. And make sure the gelatin is firm before unmolding it. Depending on how deep the mold is, it may take several hours in the refrigerator.

To unmold gelatin, you will need to have the serving plate ready. Put the plate face down on top of the mold and flip the whole thing over. The gelatin should plop out onto the plate. If it doesn't come right out of the mold, give it some help. But don't run a lot of hot water over the mold or dip it in a pan of hot water to loosen the gelatin. That will melt enough gelatin so that it will run all over your plate. Just give the mold a shake or carefully loosen the edges with a table knife. If necessary, dip a dishcloth in some hot water, wring it out, and lay it on top of the upside-down mold for a moment until you feel the gelatin plop out.

Now you can get creative. Why not surround that shimmering gelatin heart with a medley of fruits? You could ring it with slices of red apple and put red grapes on top of the apple slices. Or use defrosted frozen fruit like whole strawberries and cherries. Think about what kinds of fruits will look pretty, and use a combination of fresh, frozen, and canned fruits to design an inviting taste treat.

Top the whole thing off with whipped cream, and if you use the kind that comes in a pressurized can, you can draw a lacy Valentine heart that will be the finishing touch to your gorgeous dessert.

Passionate Pink Sorbet

In case you didn't know it, sorbet (pronounced sor-BAY) is a fancy name for fruit sherbet or ice. This is an impressive and truly delicious dessert, and no one will believe that it was so quick and easy to make.

2 cups of fresh or frozen fruit
¼ cup of water
¼ cup of sugar
1 tablespoon of lemon juice
blender or food processor

You can use any kind of fresh or frozen fruit you want so long as it's peeled and cored or pitted. But for Valentine's Day, frozen strawberries are just the thing. Don't get the kind that are in syrup—buy the ones that come in a bag and have no sugar added.

Fill a two-cup measure with frozen berries and let them sit on the counter to thaw for a half hour or so—it's hard to run them through the blender when they are as solid as rocks.

To make the sorbet, put the berries, sugar, water, and lemon juice into the blender or food processor (ask an adult for help or permission to use the machine). Blend it until it's all slushy—this only takes half a minute or so. Pour the mixture into a bowl or plastic container or ice cube tray (without the dividers) and put it in the freezer for about an hour. Then take it out and blend it again until smooth.

Put it back into the freezer. If you've made it several days in advance, put it in a covered container. But if you're serving it soon, you can refreeze it in the serving bowl so it's ready to take to the table.

And be prepared to get lots of compliments—this sorbet is as pretty as it is yummy. You won't have any leftovers of this dessert!

Do-It-Yourself Frozen Yogurt

This is another frozen fruit dessert that's made in the blender but with quite a different flavor. It's just as easy to make as the sorbet and it tastes just as good.

1 cup of plain yogurt
1 cup of frozen strawberries
4 tablespoons of sugar
cupcake tin and 8 paper liners
shredded coconut for decoration (optional)

Let the strawberries thaw completely and then dump the yogurt, berries, and sugar into the blender or food processor (make sure you have an adult's help

FREEZE
TWO
HOURS

or permission to use the machine). It takes no more than a minute to blend it all together into a frothy pink concoction.

Put the paper liners into the cupcake tin and pour equal amounts of the fruit-yogurt blend into them. Put the tin into the freezer for a couple of hours until the mixture is frozen.

Of course, you can just serve these individual frozen yogurts plain, but it's simple to create a festive Valentine look. Turn out the yogurt cups onto dessert plates and remove the paper liners. Then sprinkle each one with some shredded coconut and top this "lace" with a Valentine heart-shaped candy. What a refreshing end to a heart-y dinner!

Big Sweet-Heart

No dessert says "holiday" the way cake does. This big and beautiful heart-shaped cake serves a crowd, and it's a lot of fun to make.

1 package of white cake mix
other ingredients the mix calls for
1 container of white ready-to-spread
    frosting
red food coloring
shredded coconut, cinnamon red-hots, or
    heart-shaped candies for decoration
1 round and 1 square baking pan that
    measure the same, such as an 8-inch
    diameter round cake pan and an 8-inch
    square one

Follow the package directions to mix the batter and divide it evenly between the pans. Try to fill them to the same level. Ask an adult for permission or help in using the oven. When the cakes are baked, put them on racks to cool slightly and then turn them out of their pans. Leave the cakes on racks until they are completely cool to the touch.

Put the frosting into a small bowl and mix it with a spoon while you add red food coloring a drop at a time. Three or four drops makes a pretty pastel pink, or use more if you want a rosier hue.

You'll need a giant plate to put your cake on. If you don't have anything big enough, use part of a cardboard box. The lid or side of a large corrugated carton will work well. Cover it with aluminum foil. With the cake on it, your "silver platter" will make a gorgeous centerpiece for the table.

Cut the round cake in half and place the straight sides against two adjoining sides of the square cake on the serving platter. Don't worry if the cakes don't exactly match up; you'll even them off with frosting.

Spoon out the frosting onto the cake and spread it all over the top and sides with a table knife.

Smothered in pink frosting, this huge heart cake looks as pretty as a picture. And if you want to dress it up even more, you can edge it with shredded coconut, cinnamon red-hots, or heart-shaped candies with Valentine sayings on them.

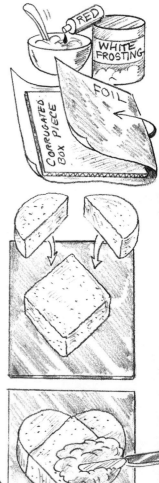

· PINK DRINKS ·

Of course you'll want to serve pink drinks to enhance the Valentine look. Think about the rest of your meal and what would go with it. Do you want hot drinks in mugs or cool ones in tall, cold glasses? Do you like the idea of a tart drink or would you prefer something sweeter? Take a look at the suggestions that follow and then you can decide.

Hot and Spicy

Nothing tastes better than a mug of hot red cider on a blustery February day.

cranberry juice
apple juice
5 or 6 whole cloves
2 or 3 cinnamon sticks
a handful of raisins

In a saucepan combine equal amounts of cranberry and apple juice with the cloves, cinnamon sticks, and raisins. Heat the mixture through, but don't boil it (make sure you have permission to use the stove). Use a ladle and be cautious with this hot cider. Serve it in mugs and put a few of the raisins in each one.

Tall, cool, and delicious are the words for this creative selection of drinks.

    assorted red and pink fruit juices (cranberry,
       raspberry, pink grapefruit, and red juice
       blends)
    orange juice
    pink lemonade
    ice cube trays

You are going to make ice cubes out of one or two of the juices, so decide on what combinations will look best. How about pink grapefruit juice in a glass filled with bright red raspberry ice cubes? Or wouldn't a glass of cranberry juice look festive with orange ice cubes floating in it?

Simply fill ice cube trays with the juices you decide to have as cubes. They won't freeze to the same rock-hardness that plain water does, so keep them in the freezer until you're ready to put them into the glasses and serve. Then let all your friends choose the ones they want.

Fizzy and Fun

This is a simple way to add some pizzazz to a plain fruit drink.

> bright red fruit juice
> club soda or seltzer
> slices of lemon, lime, or orange
> ice cube tray

Make juice ice cubes with the same or a contrasting juice, according to your mood. When the cubes are frozen, mix equal amounts of red juice and club soda in a tall glass and add the juice cubes. Float a thin slice of lemon, orange, or lime on top of the drink for a festive look.

Smooth and Creamy

How about a dessert you can drink? This wonderfully thick milkshake is the perfect ending to a Valentine meal.

    strawberry ice cream
    milk
    red food coloring, strawberry jam, or
        frozen strawberries (optional)
    blender

Put a big scoop of ice cream and a cup or so of milk into the blender. Just one drop of red food coloring will heighten the pink tone. And you can spark up the flavor by adding a spoonful of strawberry jam or a few frozen berries. Blend it all until the shake is thick and creamy (make sure you're allowed to use the blender). Then serve the milkshake in a tall glass with a couple of straws and get ready to make seconds.

What did the boy octopus say to the girl octopus?

Can I hold your hand, hand, hand, hand, hand, hand, hand, hand?

What did one snake say to the other snake?

Give me a little hug and a hiss, honey.

·5· *A Perfect Day for a Party*

What could be a more appropriate way to celebrate Valentine's Day than to have friends gather for fun and food? Share the pleasure of planning the party with a few pals, and you'll all have a chance to be creative and try out your wildest ideas.

Once you've decided on the time and place, the first thing you'll need to do is send out some invitations. And of course you'll want to plan the look of the party as well as what sort of food you'll be serving. Are you going to ask guests to wear only red and pink and white? Do you plan to have party favors, or how about a prize of some sort? Getting together to prepare for the party will be almost as much fun as the party itself.

· YOU'RE INVITED ·

Is there an old incomplete deck of cards lying around? If so, they can become part of your invitations. Pull out all the hearts. Since there are thirteen of them in a deck and you will be cutting them in half, you'll have enough for twenty-six guests (but you don't have to invite that many!).

You need one card for every two people who will be at the party (don't forget to count yourself). Cut each card in two in a jagged line and put one piece in each invitation. These card halves will be used at the party to pair people up for a quiz game.

For each invitation you also need an envelope (use the kind you bought for Nifty Notepaper, page 38) and a 3-by-5-inch index card. On the card use red ink to print the information—date, time, place, etc.—and tell your guests to be sure to bring their half playing cards with them to the party. If you decide on a costume party, this is the place to say so.

Here's a sample invitation:

A VALENTINE'S DAY PARTY
AT BETSY'S HOUSE
Saturday, February 14th, 5-9 P.M.
♥ Your ticket is enclosed—no admittance without it!
♥ Valentine outfits required (red, white, or pink)
FUN! GAMES! PRIZES! FOOD!
See you there!
RSVP - 765-4321

Decorate the index card with heart stickers or designs and put both the index card and the half playing card in the envelope. Address the envelopes and put them in the mail a few days before the party.

· HOUSE FULL OF HEARTS ·

When you think of decorations for a Valentine's Day party, what is the first thing that springs to mind?

Hearts, of course. See how many ways you can think of to festoon your house with hearts.

How about a curtain of crepe paper streamers hanging over the doorway to the party room? The streamers could be of varying lengths and each could have a red construction paper heart stapled to its end.

If helium-filled balloons are easy for you to get, tie bunches of them on long strings to chair arms and other low pieces of furniture. Have a few float loose against the ceiling with small hearts tied to the ends of their strings. If you are using regular air-filled balloons, you'll want them attached in bunches of five or six to curtain rods, hanging lamps, and other high places in the room. Either way, use red, pink, and white heart-shaped balloons, or draw red hearts in felt-tip pen on fat white and pink ones.

Naturally, you'll want to decorate your table. What could be better than a heart print runner and a tree bearing heart-y fortunes?

Instead of a tablecloth, make a runner that goes down the middle of the table from one end to the other. Use plain white shelf paper. Cut the roll to the length you need and then print red hearts all over one

SHELF PAPER
TABLE RUNNER

side of the runner with a cutout sponge and poster paint (see page 28 for how to do this).

For the fortune tree you need a branch that you can stand up in a flowerpot full of dirt. Wrap red tissue paper around the flowerpot and tie a wide white ribbon around the top edge to give it a festive air. Make sure the branch is well anchored in the dirt.

Now you need to make up the fortunes. Use two small construction paper hearts for each guest. Poke a hole through both hearts and use yarn or narrow ribbon to hang them from branches of the "tree."

Before you tie them to the tree, write a fortune on the inside of one of the hearts in each pair. Think of fortunes that will appeal to your guests. If you're sure they won't be embarrassed, it might be fun to have romantic fortunes like, "You'll meet your true love on the bus next week," or "The love of your life has a name six letters long." Or you might prefer less gushy fortunes, like "Good luck will come your way soon." How about including funny ones, like "When opportunity knocks, try not to be out to lunch" or even puns, like "If you were an evergreen, I'd pine for you"?

You won't want your fortune tree centerpiece to

have bare branches too soon, so let guests pick a fortune just before they leave. It will give them something to giggle about on the way out.

What about some pretty placemats for the table? You could make them with large construction paper hearts and paper doilies, or you could buy a package of rectangular paper placemats or tray liners. They come in white or pink in a cutout doily look, or you can get plain white ones and print them to match the runner. Large round doilies come in red as well as white, and those might look nice on top of a plain white backing. Use your own imagination to come up with a look you like—the important thing is to have everything go together in a Valentine color scheme.

· WEAR YOUR HEART ON YOUR SLEEVE ·

There are lots of ways to jazz up your clothes for Valentine's Day. Start with any combination of red, pink, and white—red running pants and a white shirt or sweatshirt, or a pink turtleneck with a white skirt or painter's pants. Once you have your basic outfit, you can start adding to it.

How about "wearing your heart on your sleeve"? This is a very old expression—it was used by Shakespeare in the play *Othello,* which is all about love and jealousy. Nowadays, if someone says you are wearing your heart on your sleeve, it means you are being very obvious about who you love, and usually it means you love that person in vain. It might be kind of funny to put a heart sticker on the sleeve of your shirt for the party and see if anyone recognizes the expression.

Stickers are great for ornamenting your clothes. Attach them to a T-shirt in a necklace design or a heart outline. Make a Victorian choker (see page 46), but tie it around your head so the heart is in the middle of your forehead. Or decorate a long neck chain with heart stickers back to back—they'll look like charms. You could even make a belt out of a piece of ribbon sandwiched between several pairs of heart stickers. Think of ways to make hair ornaments with ribbon or lacy seam binding and stickers—and don't forget to put stickers on your shoes.

For a more costumed look, make this easy heart sandwich board to wear over your shoulders. To draw a neat pattern, find a plate or bowl that measures about eight inches across. Trace around its rim on scratch paper. Cut out the traced circle and then fold and cut it in half. Measure the straight edge of one half

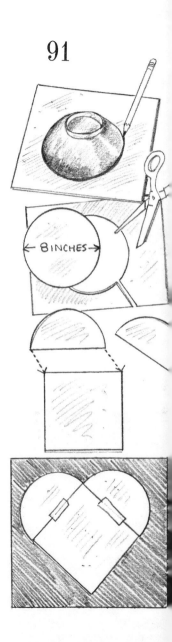

circle and then draw and cut out a square with sides that length. Tape the pattern together—it should cover your front from your shoulders to somewhere near your waist.

Trace the heart pattern twice on red lightweight cardboard and cut both hearts out. Hold one heart up to your shoulders and mark with pencil the places where the straps should go. With a paper punch, make holes where you've marked the hearts. Ribbon or yarn or even string will make straps for your sandwich board—ask someone to help you tie them to the right length. Now you're ready to be a walking valentine.

· WHO'S YOUR VALENTINE? ·

Involving your guests in a game is a good way to get your party going. Have a pile of papers ready for when people arrive. Each paper should have the name of half of a famous pair—Romeo and Juliet, Bert and Ernie, Jack and Jill, Clark Kent and Lois Lane, Shake and Bake, Up and Down, or whatever others you come up with—the sillier the better.

Without letting them see what's on the papers, pin one name to the back of each guest's shirt. Then let everyone try to find out what his or her name is and

who is the other half of the pair. Tell your guests they can ask any questions they want as long as the answer can be simply "yes" or "no."

When everyone is identified, it's time for another game. For this one too, you'll have to prepare things in advance. Your guests will match their playing card halves to find their partners. Then you'll all play your own version of a TV game show. Choose one that is played with partners and adapt it to your living room. For instance, use whistles instead of buzzers or bang on tinfoil pans for the end of a round. Try a spinner from a board game instead of a big wheel, and make up your own questions or borrow some from a question-and-answer type game. Take turns being the host or hostess—the people who are waiting to play get to be the studio audience.

For all your game prizes and for party favors, try to think of things that are inexpensive and funny. Carry out the Valentine theme with heart-shaped erasers and pencils, packages of heart stickers, small sacks of candy hearts with sayings on them, or whatever else appeals to you. Look in novelty and discount stores for ideas, and make sure there's a small gift for everyone to take home.

It's Valentine's Day at last. You've made the house look gorgeous and put on your own Valentine outfit. You've gotten all the food ready—maybe it's heart-shaped pizza and an assortment of terrific desserts. While you're waiting for your guests to arrive, there's one more thing you can do to create the party atmosphere. Put about a dozen whole cloves, a broken cinnamon stick, and a few pieces of lemon or orange in a large pan of water. With an adult's permission, set it on the stove and let it come to a boil. Then turn the heat way down and leave the pan to simmer quietly during the party. (Now and then check to make sure that the water hasn't boiled away.) The delicious scent will waft through the house like a valentine in the air.

Before you know it, the games are over and the prizes are handed out. Every bite of the fabulous Valentine food you made has disappeared and it's time for your guests to leave. As they troop out the door, it will make you feel good to hear, "This was the greatest Valentine party ever!"

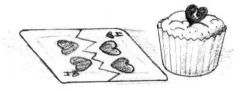

Index